Beads of sweat began
forming on Rafflesia's skin.
"Nnn... Nnn... Nnn... Nnn...
How is it, Your Majesty?"

...Someone barged into the dining hall. *"Diablo?!"* Rem appeared, raising her voice while wearing her sleeping gown.

How *NOT* to Summon a Demon Lord

Demon Lord

VOLUME 8

Yukiya Murasaki
Illust. Takahiro Tsurusaki

Rafflesia S Orangewood

Chief and priestess of the dark elves.
Has *giga* boobs.

Drango

Has the appearance of an orc, but is the
astute chancellor of the elven kingdom.
Secretly a flat chest aficionado.

Klem

The Demon Lord Krebskulm who
was sealed within Rem's body.
Surprisingly took the form of a
young, biscuit-loving girl upon
revival. Lives in Faltra, pretending
to be a member of the races.

Edelgard

A Fallen who endeavored to revive
Klem. Works at a bakery to
finance her Demon Lord's
biscuit-guzzling ways.

CHARACTERS

Diablo

A top player of a game very similar to this world. He is in fact socially inept, and can't communicate without acting the part of his in-game character. AKA: "The Demon Lord from Another World"

Rem Galleu

A Pantherian summoner. The Demon Lord Krebskulm was sealed in her body, but she finally removed her after much hardship. Serious to a fault.

Shera L Greenwood

Princess of the Elves. Choosing Diablo as the king of her country, she finally became queen. Claims to be a summoner, but is a much more skilled archer. Speaks in a light, easygoing fashion.

How NOT to Summon a Demon Lord: Volume 8
by Yukiya Murasaki

Translated by ZackZeal
Edited by Kris Swanson

Copyright © 2016 Yukiya Murasaki
Illustrations by Takahiro Tsurusaki

First published in Japan in 2016 by Kodansha Ltd., Tokyo.
Publication rights for this English edition arranged through Kodansha Ltd., Tokyo.

Find more books like this one at www.j-novel.club!

President and Publisher: Samuel Pinansky
Managing Editor: Aimee Zink

ISBN: 978-1-7183-5207-0
Printed in Korea
First Printing: February 2020
10 9 8 7 6 5 4 3 2 1